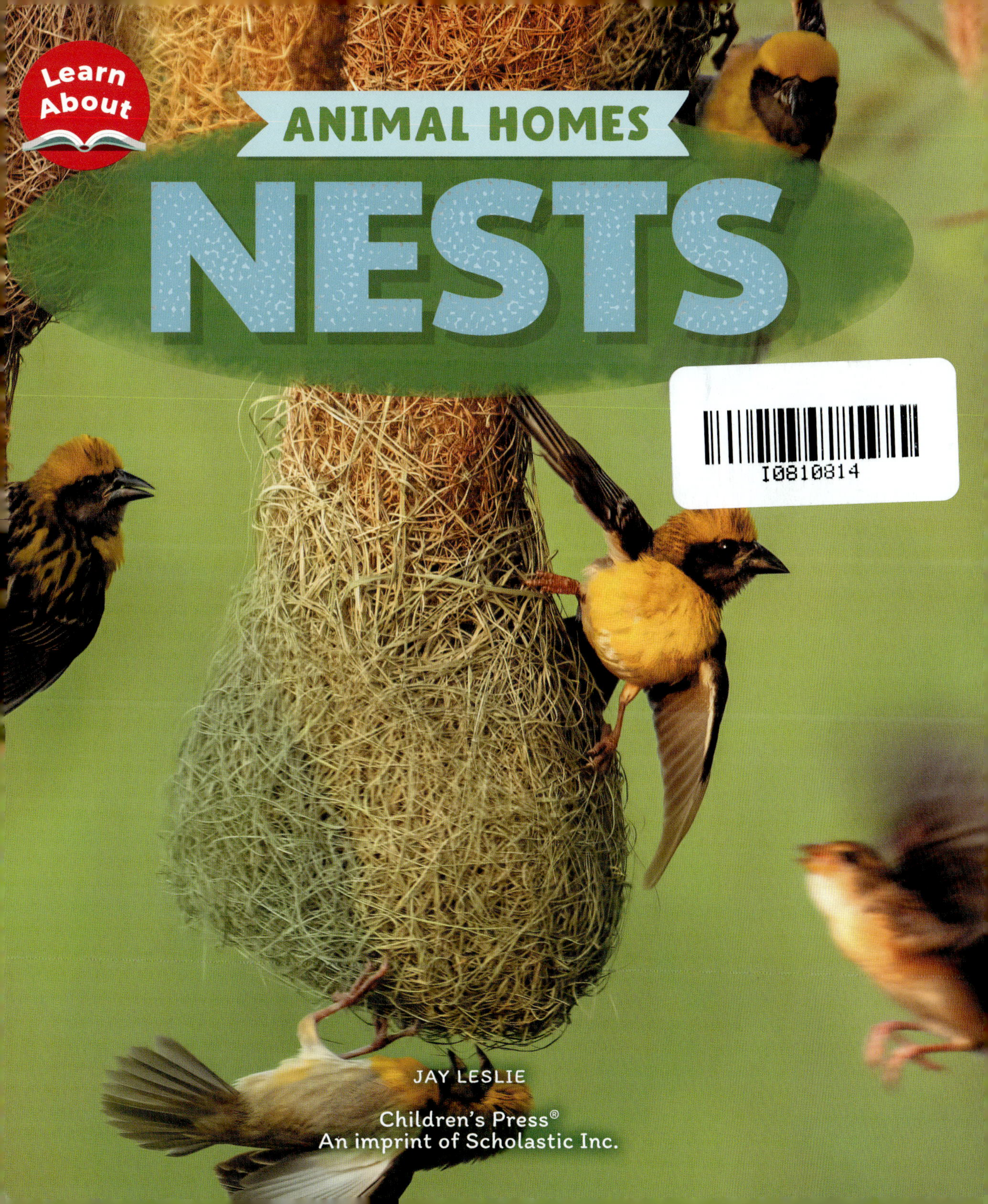

Learn About

ANIMAL HOMES

NESTS

JAY LESLIE

Children's Press®
An imprint of Scholastic Inc.

A special thank-you to the Cincinnati Zoo & Botanical Garden
for their expert consultation.

Library of Congress Cataloging-in-Publication Data available

ISBN 978-1-5461-7736-4 (library binding) | ISBN 978-1-5461-7737-1 (paperback)

10 9 8 7 6 5 4 3 2 1 26 27 28 29 30

Printed in China 62

First edition, 2026

Book design by Kay Petronio

Photos ©: cover, 1: tahir abbas/Getty Images; 6–7 background and throughout: SpicyTruffel/Getty Images; 6 bottom: Yaorusheng/Getty Images; 7 inset: Mark Newman/Getty Images; 11 main: Milaspage/Getty Images; 11 inset: Nick Bergkessel Jr./Science Source; 12–13: Michael Quinton/Minden Pictures; 13 inset: S and D and K Maslowski/FLPA/Minden Pictures; 14 top: Dorling Kindersley ltd/Alamy Images; 15 main: db_beyer/Getty Images; 16–17: Ernie Janes/Alamy Images; 17 inset: Arterra/Universal Images Group/Getty Images; 20–21: Dieter Hopf/imageBROKER/Shutterstock; 22 top: Mawaddah Fauziah/Getty Images; 23 main: pjmalsbury/Getty Images;24–25: Pete Oxford/Minden Pictures; 26: Angelique van Heertum/Alamy Images; 27: Dody Karyanto/Getty Images; 28: Shakeel Sha/Getty Images; 30: Raj Kamal/Getty Images.

CONTENTS

INTRODUCTION

COZY NESTS

A nest is a type of animal home. You might know birds build nests. But many other animals make nests, too! Squirrels gather leaves to build nests. Mice dig tunnels for their nests. Hedgehogs make sure their nests are hidden. Some frogs create foam nests for their eggs. Nests keep animals safe and warm. Animals also raise their young in nests. Let's learn how some animals make and use nests!

A hummingbird sits in her nest.

Chapter 1

BIRDS

FACT FILE

ANIMAL GROUP: Bird

DIET: Varies

HABITATS: All

FACT!

Most birds build a new nest every year. But eagles reuse their nests. They make their nests bigger over time.

Bald eagles build the biggest nests of any bird.

Birds build nests for important reasons. They need a safe place to lay their eggs and raise their chicks. A nest keeps the eggs warm. It also protects them from bad weather. It hides them from hungry predators. After the eggs hatch, the nest becomes the baby birds' home. They stay in the nest until they are strong enough to fly.

Bird nests come in all shapes and sizes. Robins weave simple cup-shaped nests in trees or shrubs. They are built from twigs, grass, and mud. Some burrowing owls dig tunnels in dirt. Their nests are underground. They can be lined with feathers or grass.

FACT!

Most types of penguins make nests. But emperor and king penguins don't. They carry their eggs on top of their feet to keep them warm.

Oriole chicks are being fed in their nest.

Nightjars barely make a nest at all! They make small dents in the ground instead. Orioles make hanging basket nests. They can use grass, string, or hair. The nests swing from tree branches like tiny hammocks.

Chapter 2

SQUIRRELS

FACT FILE

ANIMAL GROUP: Mammal

DIET: Omnivore

HABITATS: Backyards, forests, public spaces, urban areas

FACT!

Flying squirrels do not build their own nests. They move into holes that woodpeckers have made in trees.

Squirrel nests are usually high up in trees. This protects them from predators.

Have you ever seen a big messy ball of leaves in a tree? It could be a squirrel's nest! Squirrels use twigs and leaves to create a sturdy nest. Most nests are built close to a tree's trunk. The trunk is stronger and safer. Some squirrels even build more than one nest. More nests means more places to hide from predators like hawks or foxes.

In summer, squirrels build simple nests. When fall comes, they get their nests ready for winter. Or they'll build a new nest. Squirrels may line their nests with leaves, moss, and feathers.

FACT!

Eastern gray squirrels will cuddle together in their nest to stay warm.

The extra layers keep them warmer through winter. Squirrels also use their extra nests to store food. They pack away nuts and seeds.

Some squirrel nests are bigger than a basketball!

Chapter 3

MICE

FACT FILE

ANIMAL GROUP: Mammal

DIET: Omnivore

HABITATS: All

FACT!

Some deer mice build their nests with long tunnels for speedy escapes.

This mouse is well hidden in its nest.

Mice can turn almost anything into a comfy nest. They will use shredded paper, string, cardboard, and even tiny pieces of fabric. Their nests are tucked away in dark, quiet places. This could be under shrubs or inside tree stumps. Mice stay hidden from bigger animals that might want to eat them.

Mice like to be around other mice. In fact, up to 24 mice can share one nest! They also live together to keep warm in colder months. Mice may raise their babies together in their cozy nest.

FACT!

A mother mouse is in charge of the nest. She has a litter of 5 to 12 babies at a time. And she can have several litters a year!

Some mice build their nests indoors. They choose spots close to food sources like kitchens. This means they don't have to go far to find a snack. Mice like staying close to their nests.

Baby mice are born without fur. This soft nest will keep them warm.

Chapter 4

HEDGEHOGS

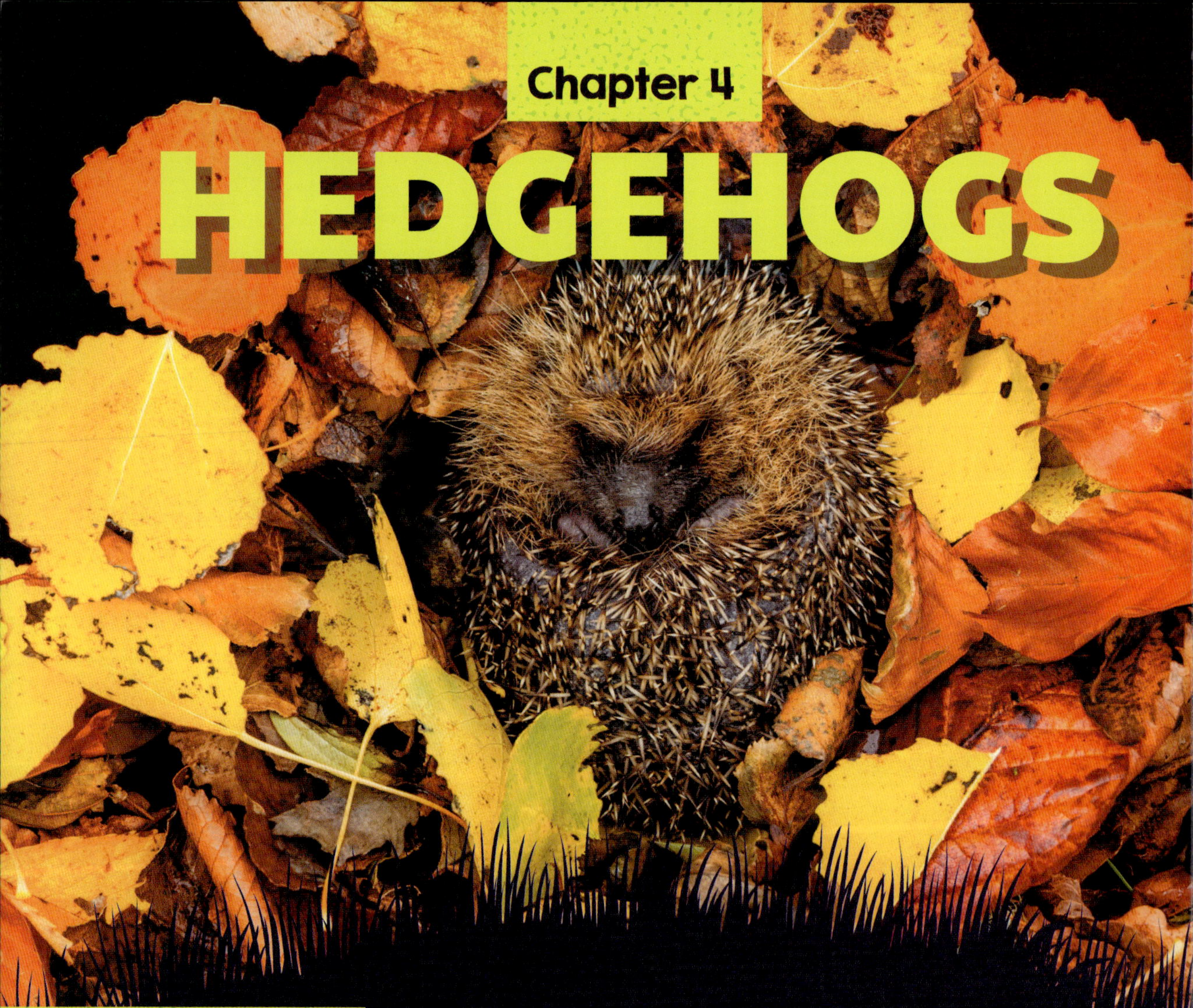

FACT FILE

ANIMAL GROUP: Mammal

DIET: Carnivore

HABITATS: Forests, gardens, grasslands

FACT!

Hedgehogs are nocturnal. They sleep in their nests during the day. They come out at night to hunt for food. Hedgehogs like to eat insects and earthworms.

Hedgehogs use moss to make their nests soft and warm.

Hedgehogs create nests for each season. In the summer, they make simple nests by gathering grass and leaves. The nests are a comfy spot to rest during the day. When winter comes, they need something bigger. They build special winter nests to hibernate in. These ball-shaped nests are packed with twigs, leaves, and other plants. They keep the hedgehog warm and dry.

Hedgehogs build their nests in safe, hidden spots. You can find them under bushes, in piles of leaves, or beneath sheds. Some hedgehogs dig nests in the ground for extra warmth during winter.

FACT!

Baby hedgehogs learn to build nests when they are three weeks old!

Hedgehogs sometimes swap nests with each other. But adults rarely share the same nest. Hedgehogs are solitary animals. That means they like to live alone.

A mother hedgehog watches over her young in their nest.

Chapter 5

FROGS

FACT FILE

ANIMAL GROUP: Amphibian

DIET: Carnivore

HABITAT: In or near fresh water

FACT!

Some tree frog foam nests can hold as many as 1,000 eggs!

This is the foam nest of a tree frog.

Different types of frogs build different kinds of nests. The foam-nest tree frog builds homes made of foam. After laying the eggs, female frogs release a special liquid. They kick it up with their back legs. The foam hardens into a covering for her eggs. These nests are usually placed right above a pond or marsh. After five days, the tadpoles hatch. They drop straight down into the water to continue growing.

Frog nests are built to keep their eggs safe. But not all frogs use foam nests. Male Limborg's frogs dig nests in the mud. They wait for a female to lay eggs in it.

This male and female frog are sharing a mud nest.

FACT!

Female poison dart frogs will eat other frogs' eggs! Fewer tadpoles means more food for her own young.

Then the males guard the eggs until they hatch. Other frogs place their nests in caves. Some frogs hide their nests in thick plants.

MORE ANIMAL NESTS

RACCOONS

Raccoons use dens as shelter and also build nests. They use nests for sleep and to protect their young. They make their nests almost anywhere. Raccoons can build nests in trees, attics, and even chimneys. Sometimes, they don't even build their own. Raccoons will take over empty squirrel or bird nests.

ALLIGATORS

Female alligators build their nests next to swamps and marshes. They are made from sticks, grass, mud, or plants. The nest hides and protects the mother's eggs. Alligator nests can be 7 to 10 feet (2 to 3 meters) wide. That is about the length of a surfboard.

SEA TURTLES

To have babies, female sea turtles crawl onto the beach. They dig small nests in the sand. They lay their eggs inside. Then they return to the ocean. The eggs hatch on their own. The hatchlings make their way to the water by themselves.

PAPER WASPS

Paper wasps chew wood and bark to make nests. Their nests look like open honeycombs. The queen lays her eggs inside. Female worker wasps take care of the eggs until they hatch. Some paper wasp nests are huge with hundreds of wasps living inside.

NESTS IN NATURE

Nests come in all shapes and sizes! You've learned about some animals that build nests. Birds weave homes with sticks and grass. Squirrels build leafy nests in branches. Mice find hidden indoor spots to make their shelters. Hedgehogs tuck their nests under bushes. And some frogs can create foamy nests. These animals all know how to make a home. The next time you're in nature, look closely. Maybe you'll spot a nest!

GLOSSARY

carnivore (KAHR-nuh-vor) an animal that eats meat

den the home of a wild animal

habitat (HAB-i-tat) the place where an animal or a plant is usually found

hatch (hach) when an egg breaks open and a baby bird or reptile comes out of it

hibernate (HYE-bur-nate) when animals sleep for the entire winter; this protects them and helps them survive when the temperatures are cold and food is hard to find

litter (LIT-ur) a number of baby animals that are born at the same time to the same mother

mammal (MAM-uhl) a warm-blooded animal that has fur and usually gives birth to live babies

nocturnal (nahk-TUR-nuhl) active at night

omnivore (AHM-nuh-vor) an animal that eats both plants and meat

predator (PRED-uh-tur) an animal that lives by hunting other animals for food

urban (UR-buhn) having to do with or living in a city

INDEX

Page numbers in **bold** indicate images.

ABOUT THE AUTHOR

Jay Leslie has always loved to write. Everywhere she goes, she carries a notebook just in case she gets a new idea. Most of all, she loves to write the books that she wishes she'd had as a child.